THE CORNERSTONE OF LITERACY

BASIC FOUNDATION

BY

CYNTHIA R. ANDERSON

TO MY GRANDCHILDREN

MAKE EVERY CHALLENGE PART OF A SOLID FOUNDATION

    Children are being taught so much so fast today, that it may become difficult for some to comprehend. This book may assist in relieving them of some of the stress involved in cursive writing. Each letter is broken down so that anyone can learn it in parts. Each stroke is practiced several times. Repetition makes it retention of writing easier.

    This book is written for all ages especially those experiencing writing illiteracy, preschoolers, kindergarten students, and those of other languages (ESL) that would like to learn to write in cursive. As students practice these skill, it will enhance their literacy as an English Language Learner.

No part of this publication may be reproduced in whole or in part, or stored in a retrieval system, or transmitted in any form or by any means, electronic, mechanical, photocopying, etc, without written permission from the author.

Copyright 2013

Trace the first part of uppercase cursive letter a

Part 1

Trace uppercase cursive letter *a*

1 2 3
Add part 2 & 3

Trace this part of uppercase cursive letter B

Part 1

Trace this part of uppercase cursive letter P

Add part 2

Trace this part of uppercase cursive letter $\mathcal{B}$

1 2 3

Add part 3

Trace this part of uppercase cursive letter $\mathcal{B}$

1 2 3 4

Add part 4

Trace uppercase cursive letter C

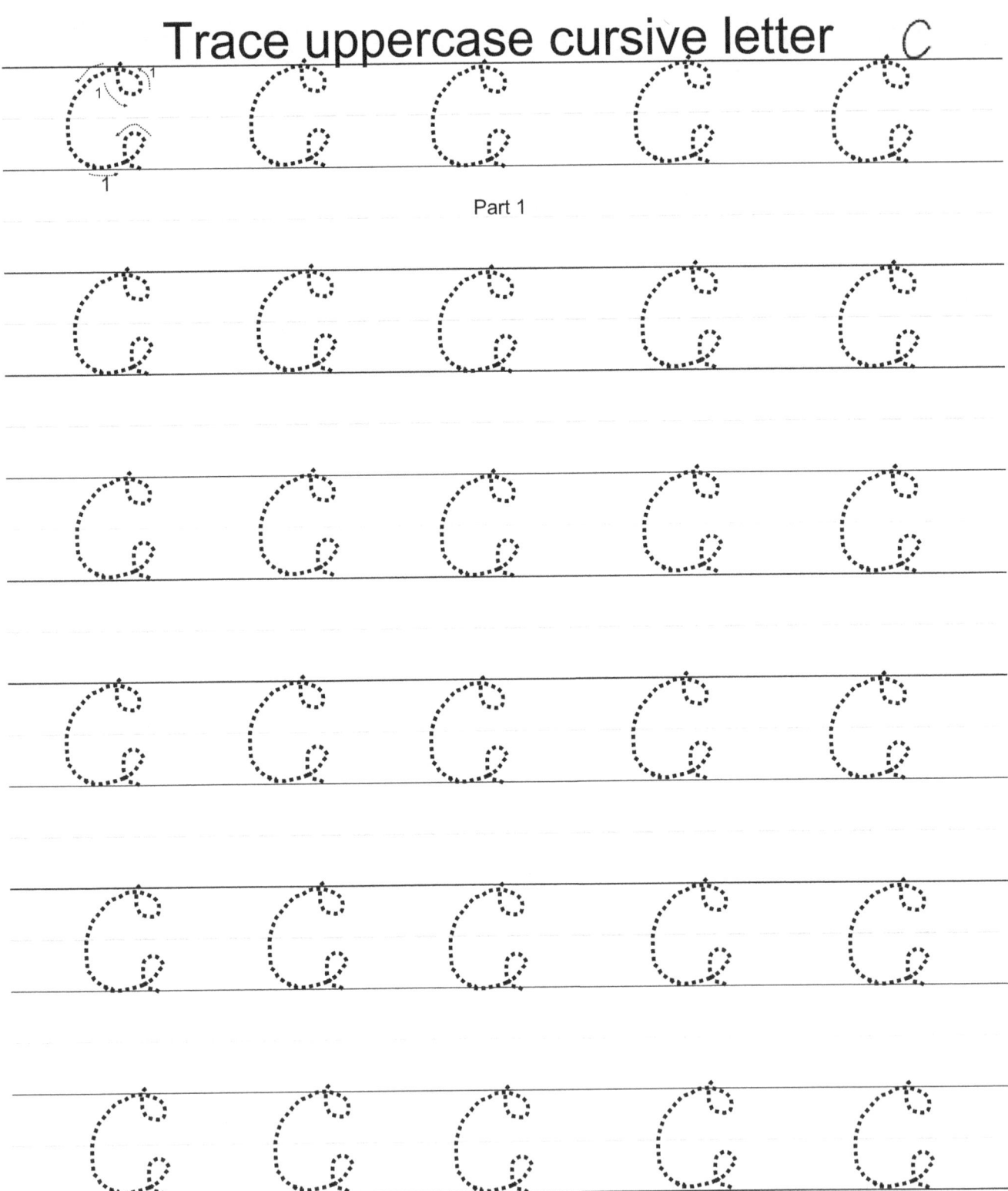

Part 1

Trace this part of uppercase cursive letter ℒ

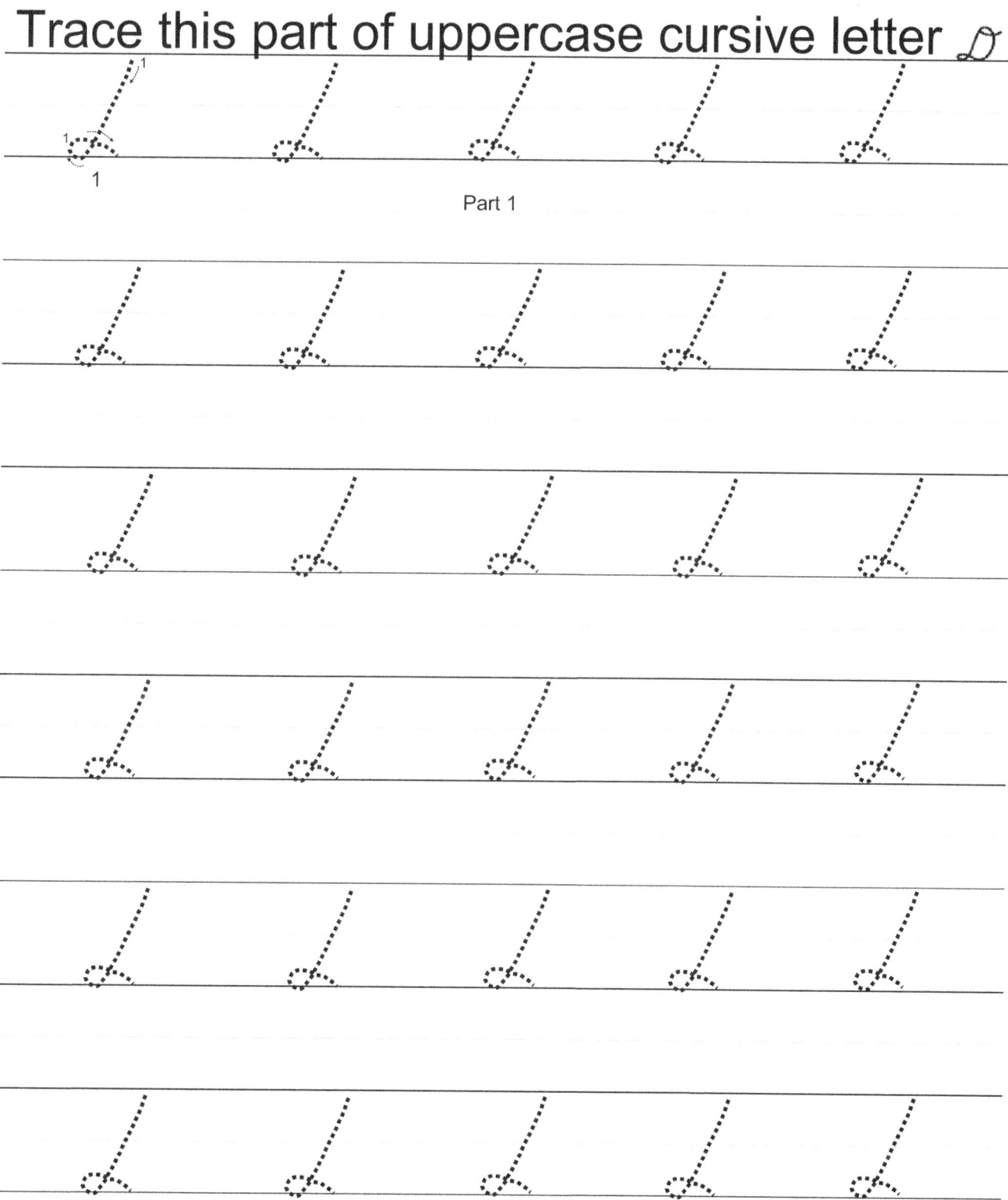

Part 1

Trace this part of uppercase cursive letter 𝒟

Add part 2

Trace uppercase cursive letter $\mathcal{D}$

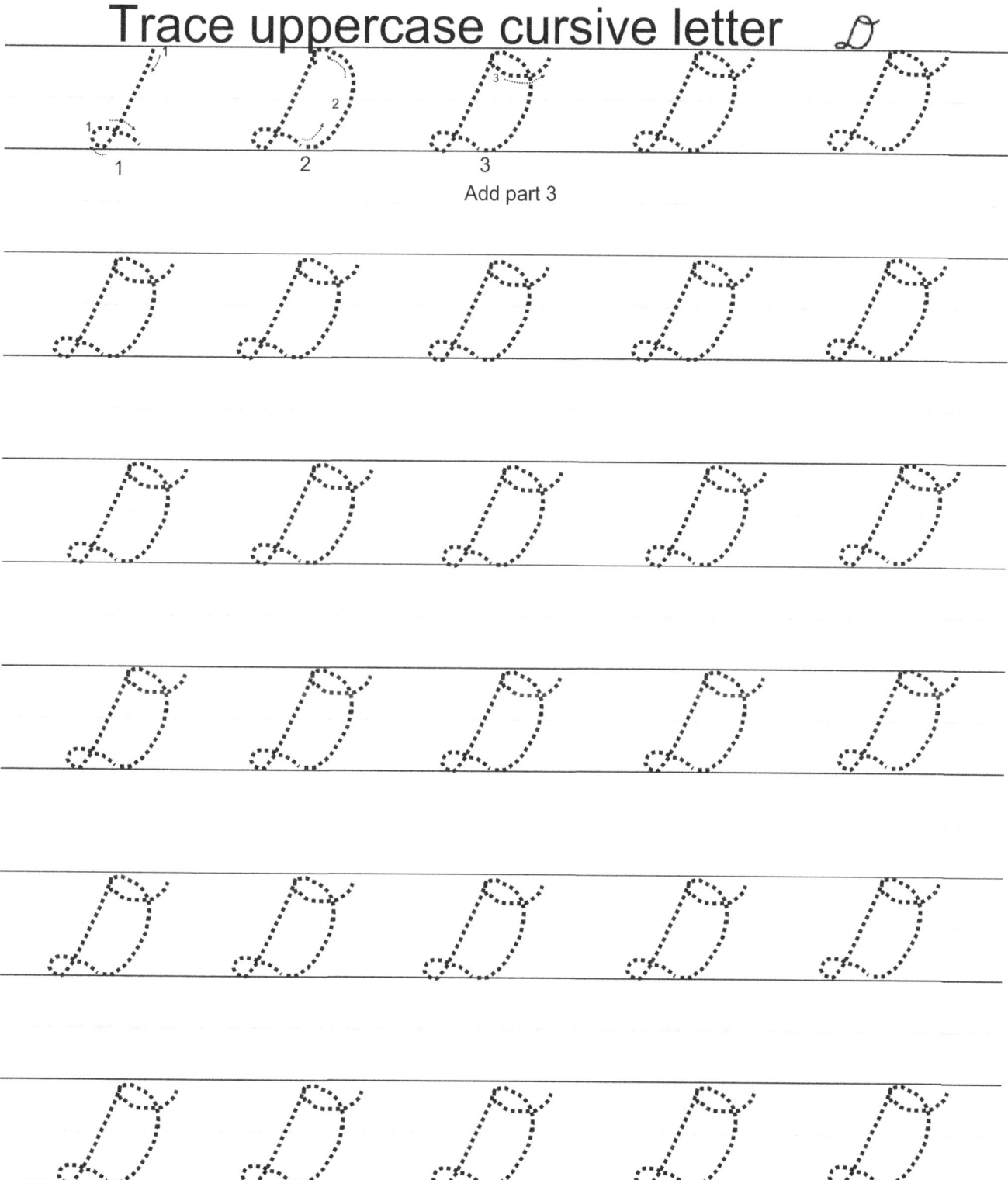

Add part 3

Trace this part of uppercase cursive letter $\mathcal{E}$

Part 1

Trace uppercase cursive letter ℰ

Add part 2

Trace this part of uppercase cursive letter 𝓕

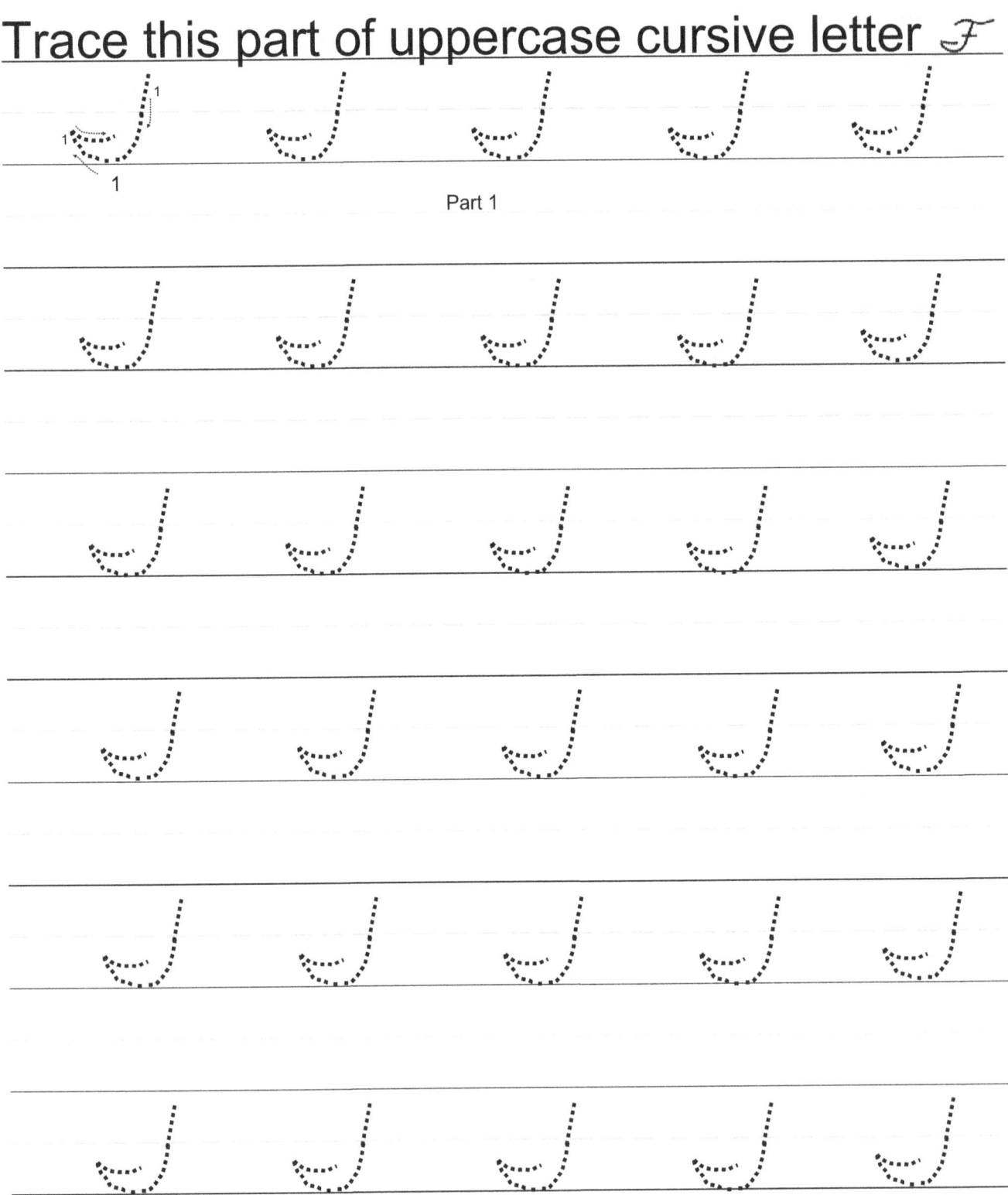

Part 1

Trace this part of uppercase cursive letter 𝓕

Add part 2

Trace uppercase cursive letter

Trace this part of uppercase cursive letter G

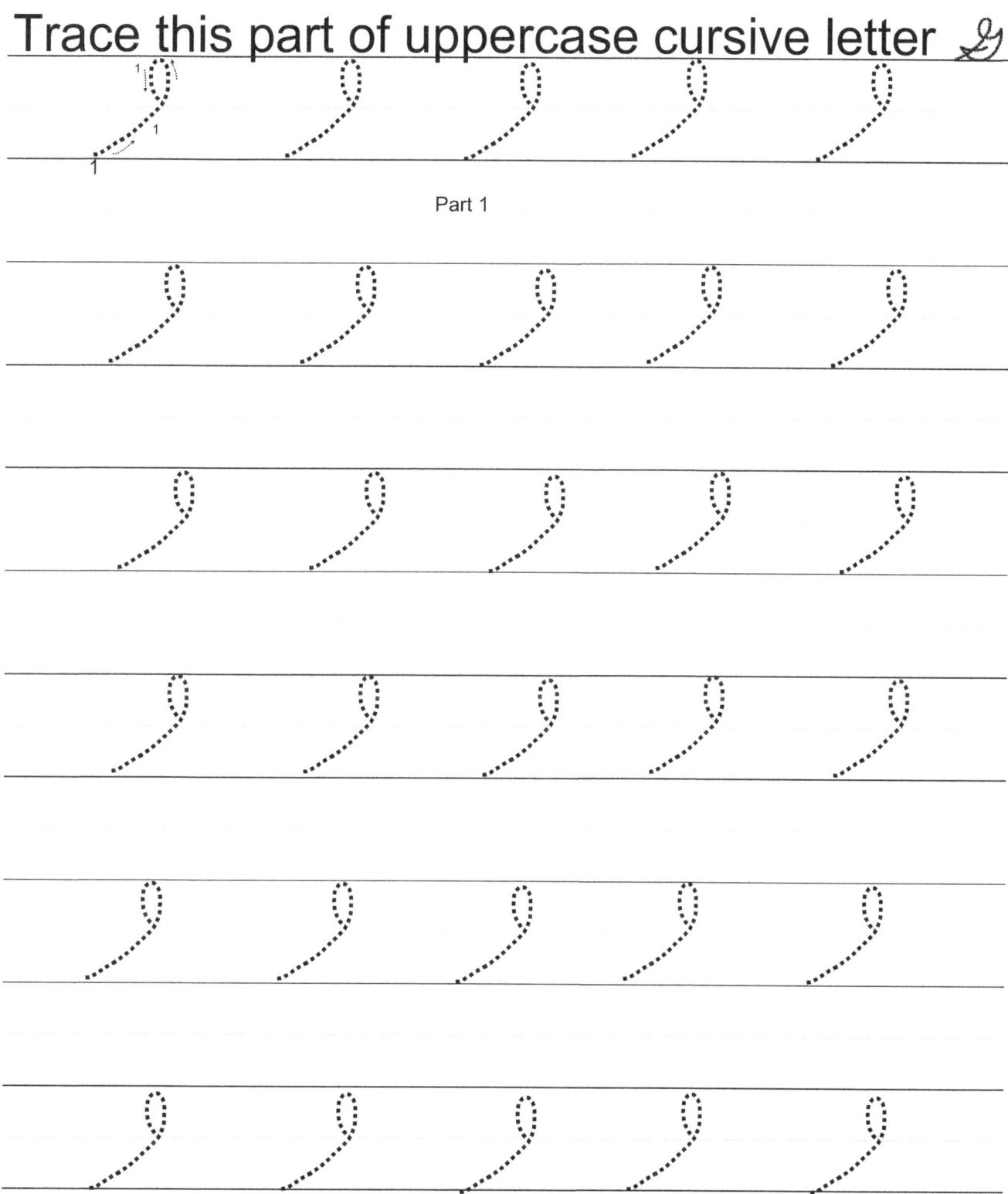

Part 1

Trace this part of uppercase cursive letter

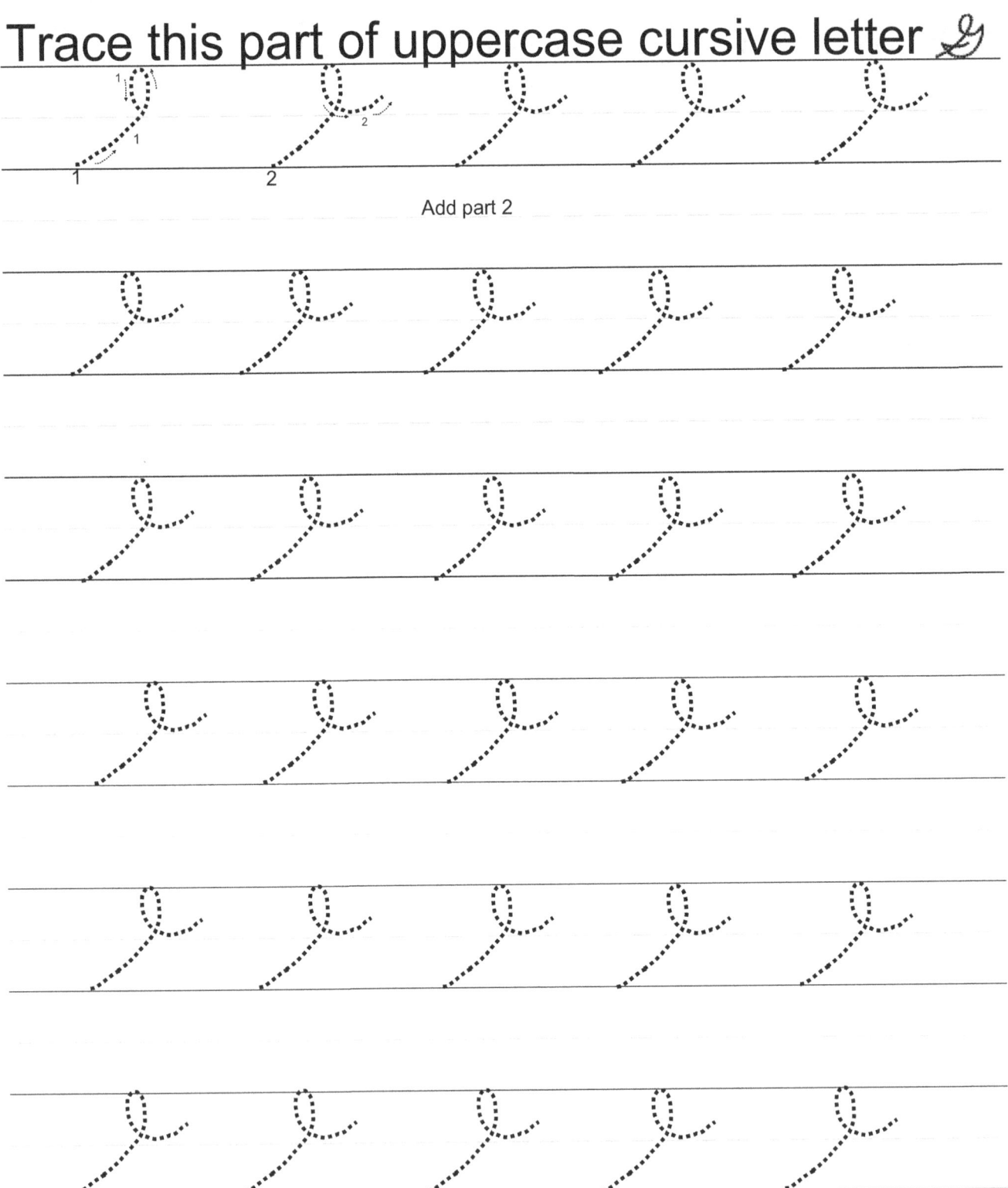

Add part 2

20

Trace this part of uppercase cursive letter ℐ

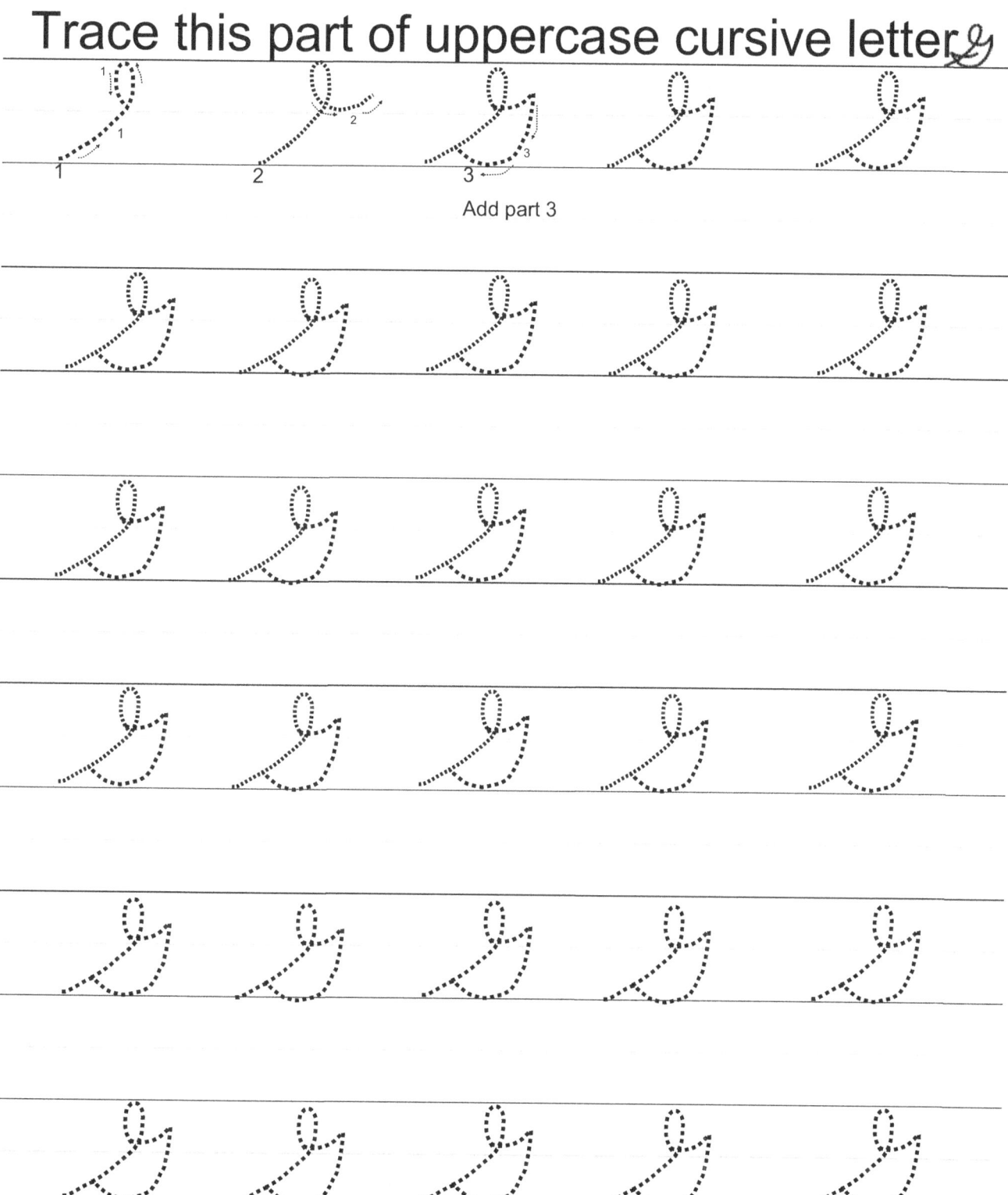

Add part 3

Trace uppercase cursive letter 𝒢

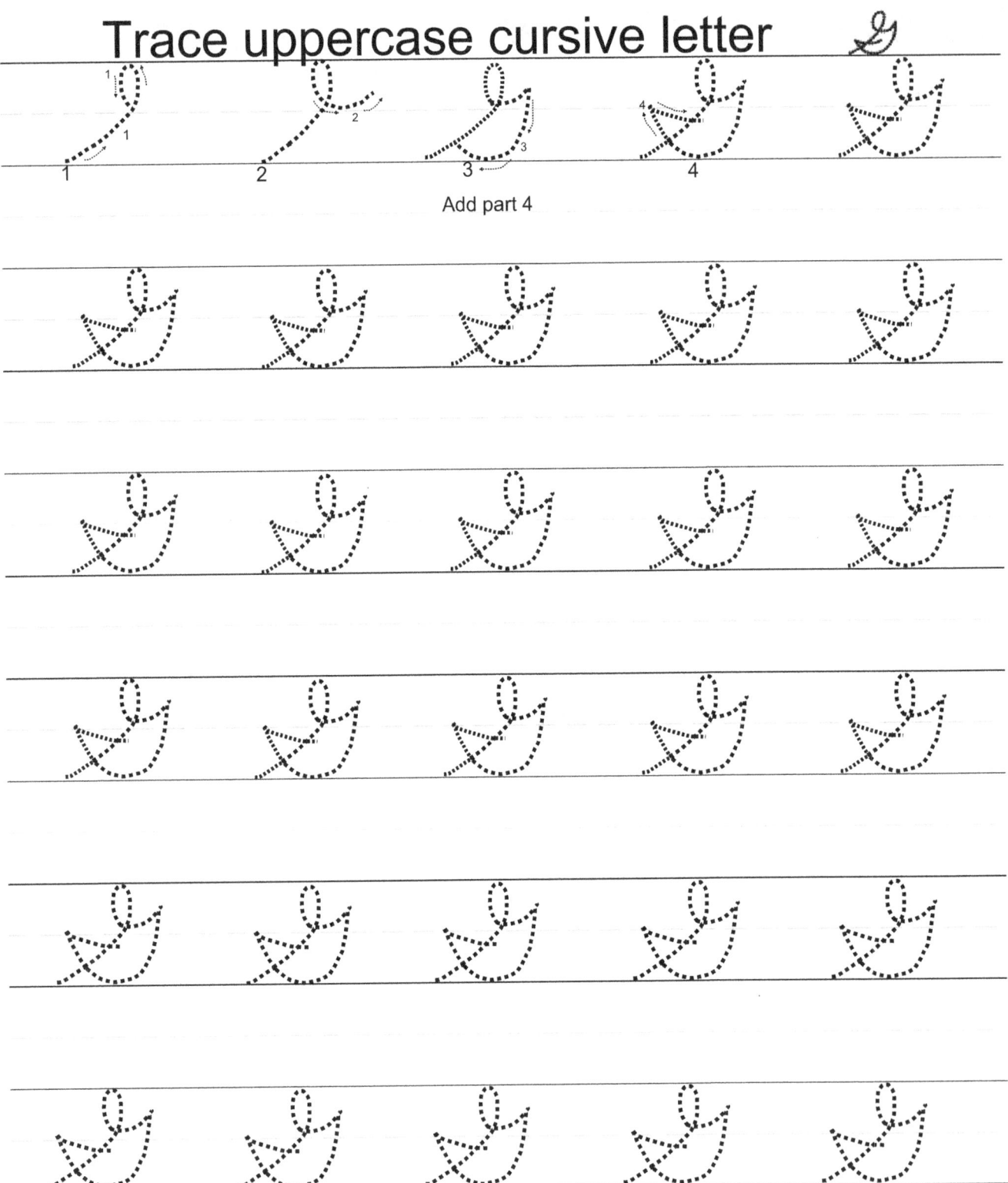

Add part 4

Trace this part of uppercase cursive letter H

Part 1

Trace this part of uppercase cursive letter H

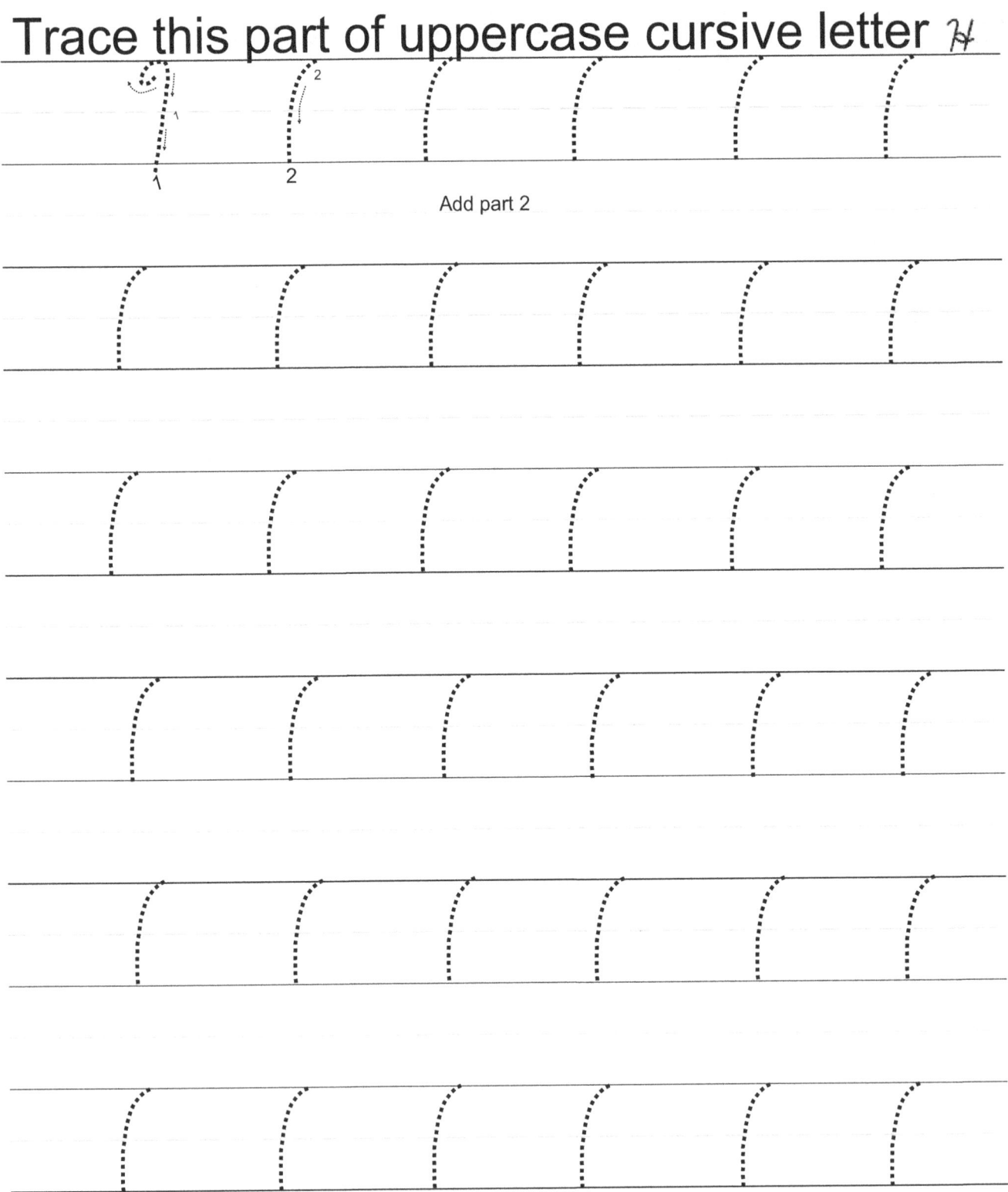

Add part 2

24

Trace this part of uppercase cursive letter H

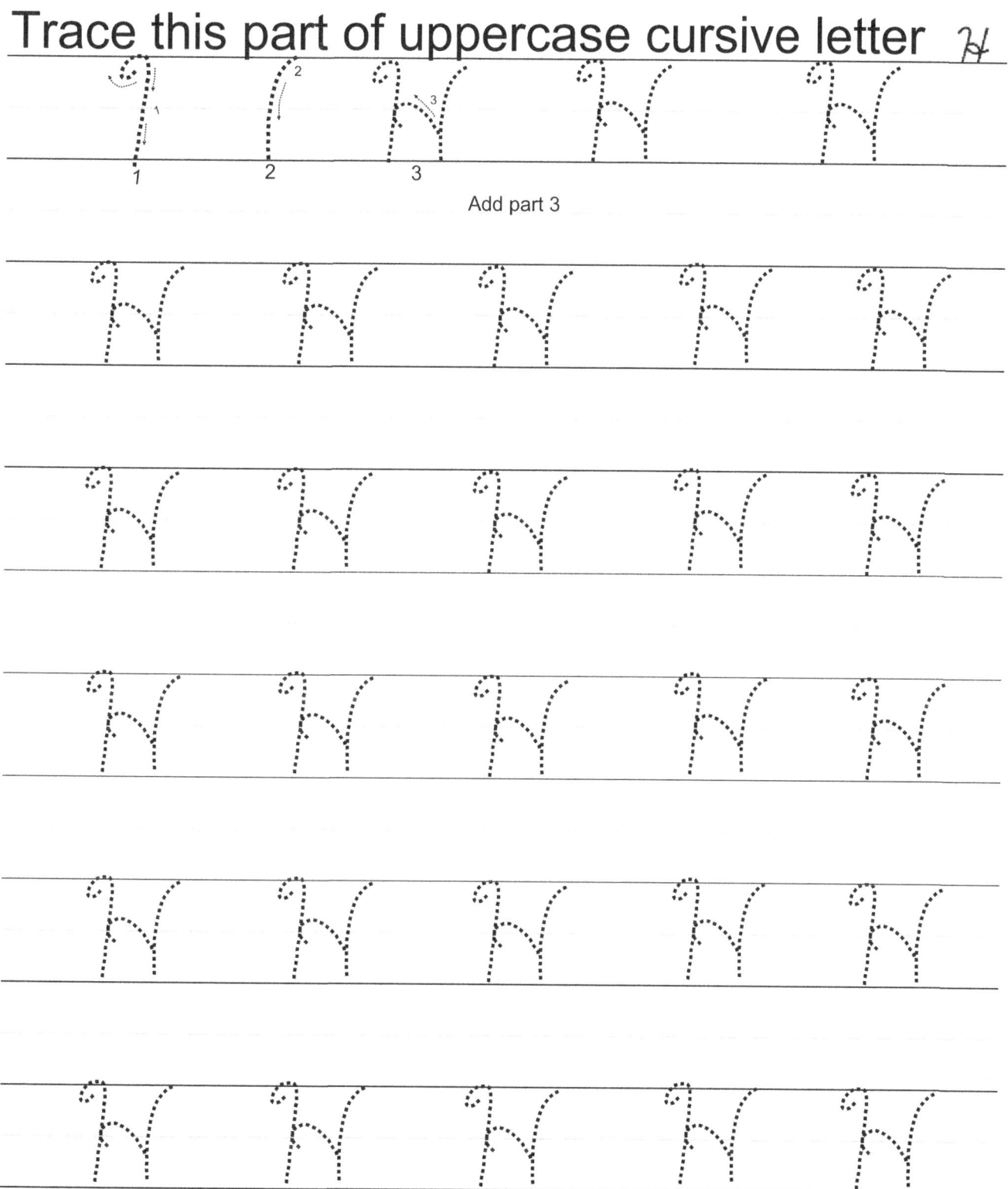

Add part 3

Trace uppercase cursive letter H

Add part 4

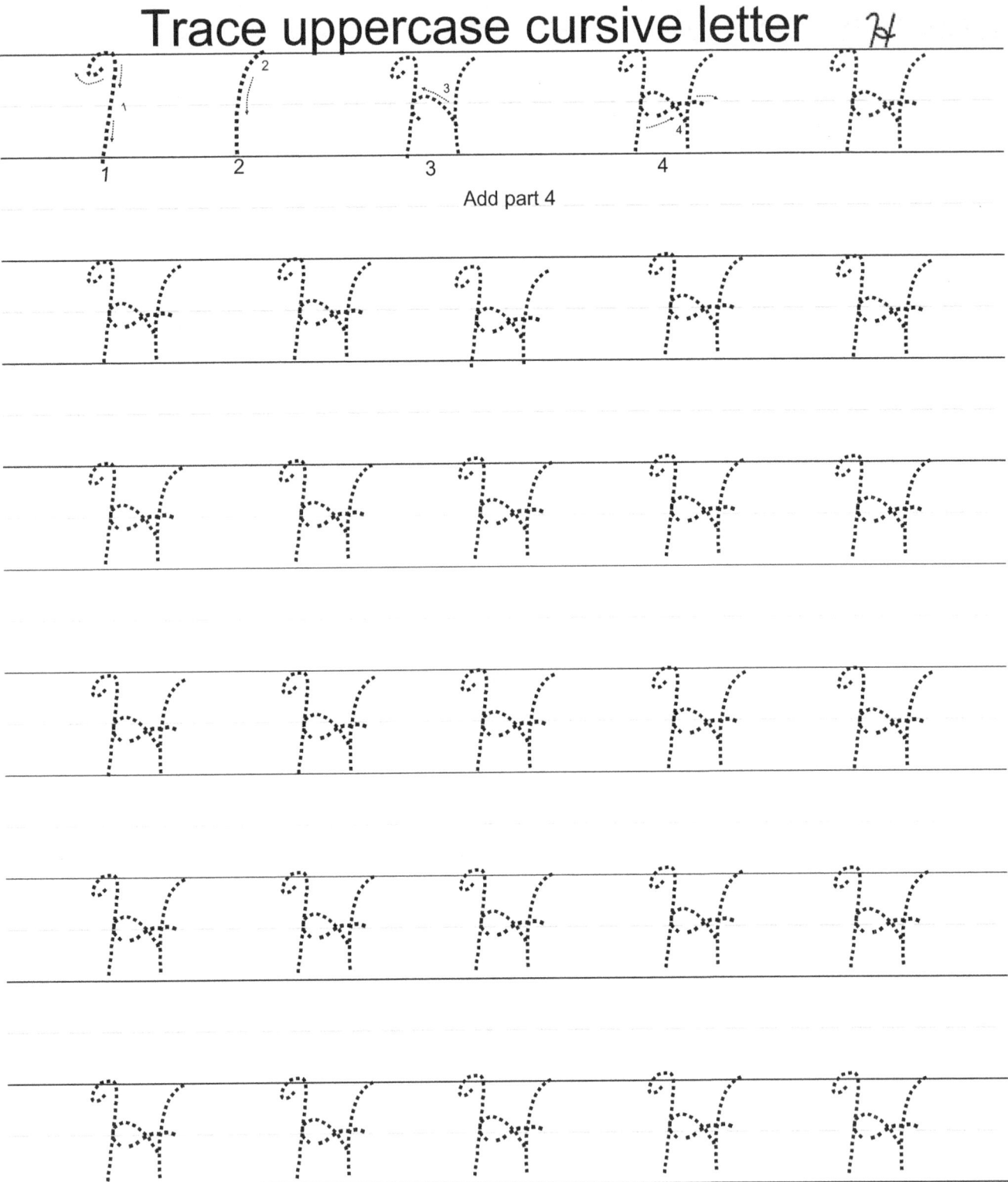

Trace this part of uppercase cursive letter ℒ

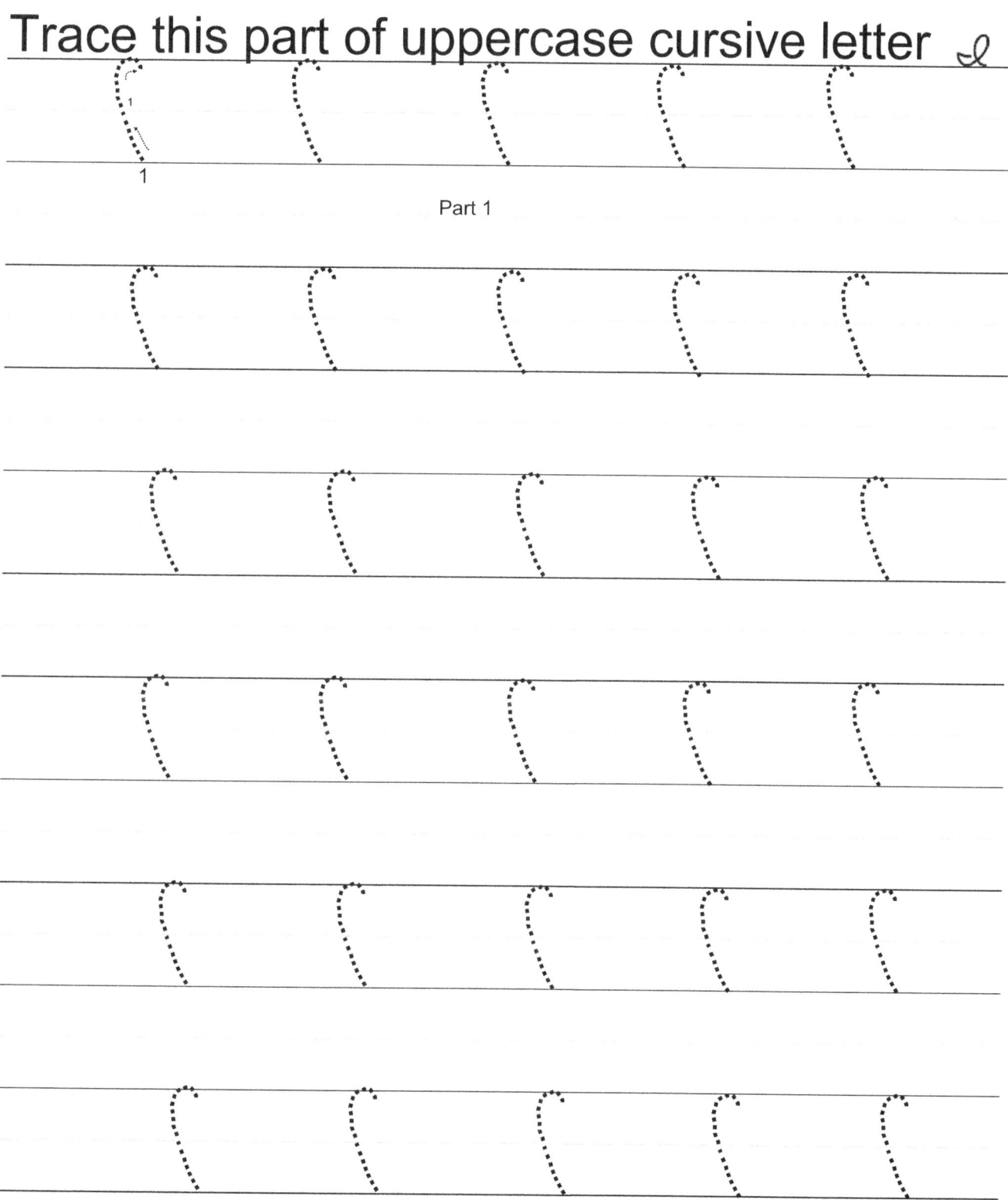

Part 1

27

Trace this part of uppercase cursive letter ℒ

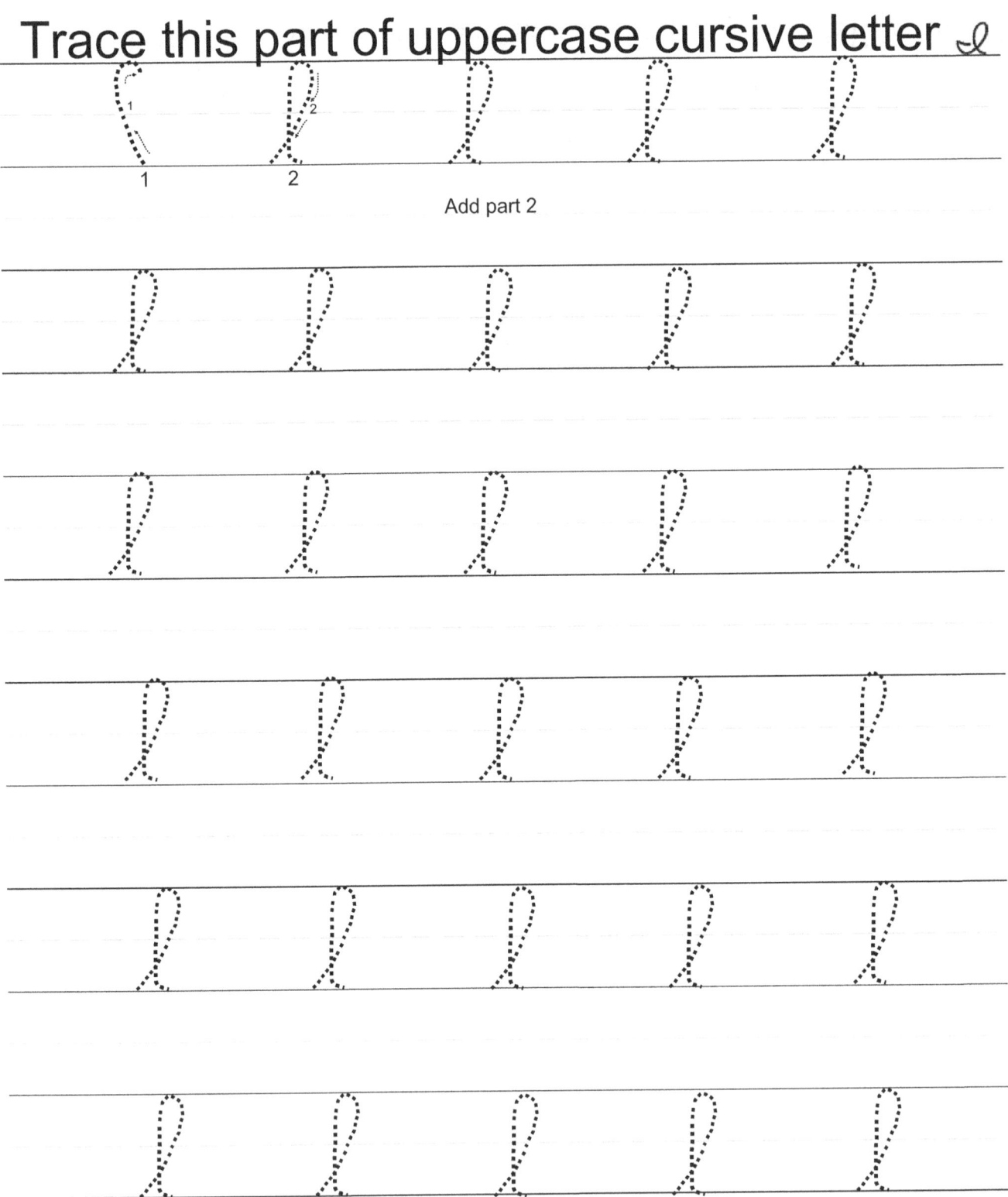

Add part 2

Trace this part of uppercase cursive letter

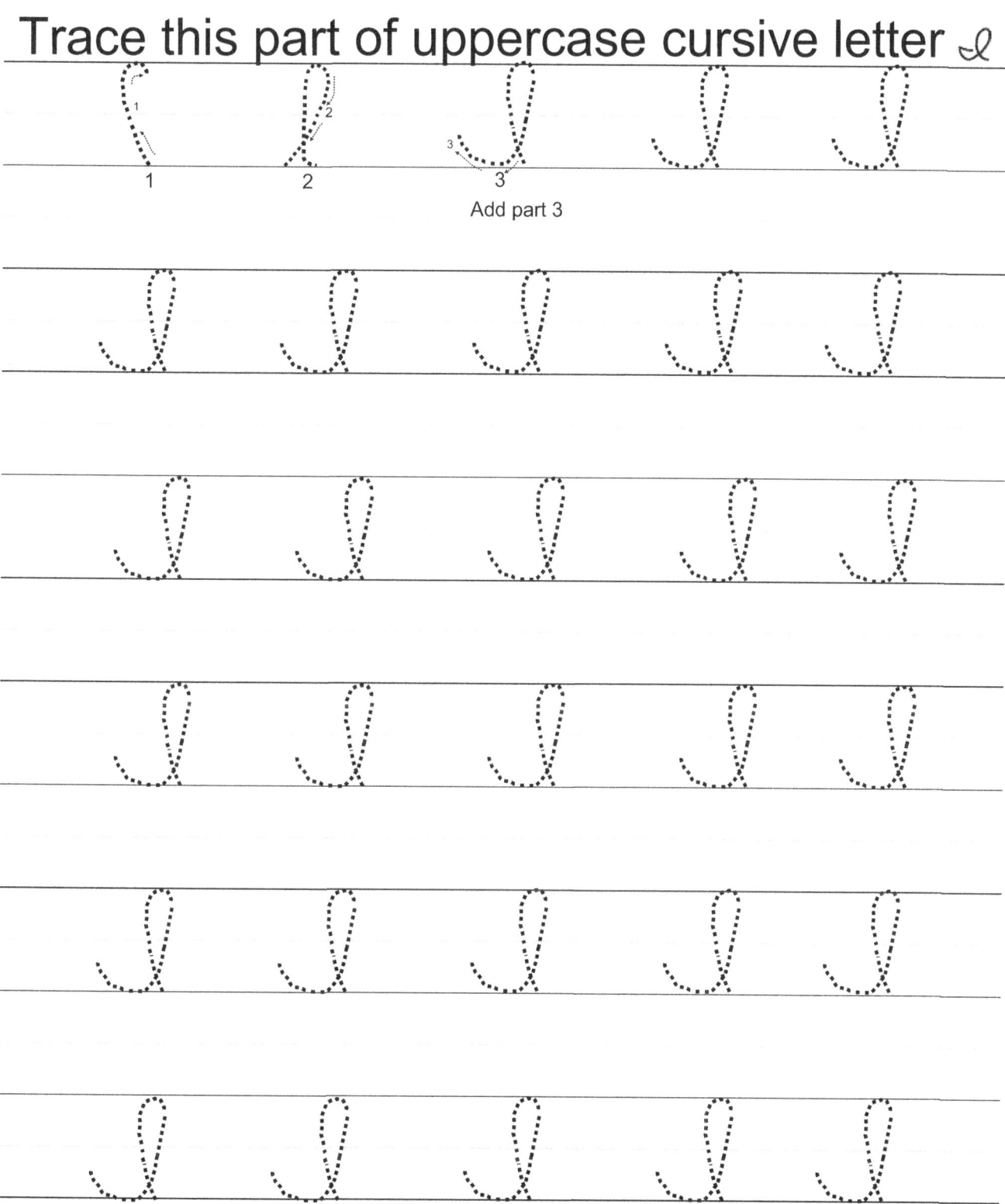

Trace uppercase cursive letter

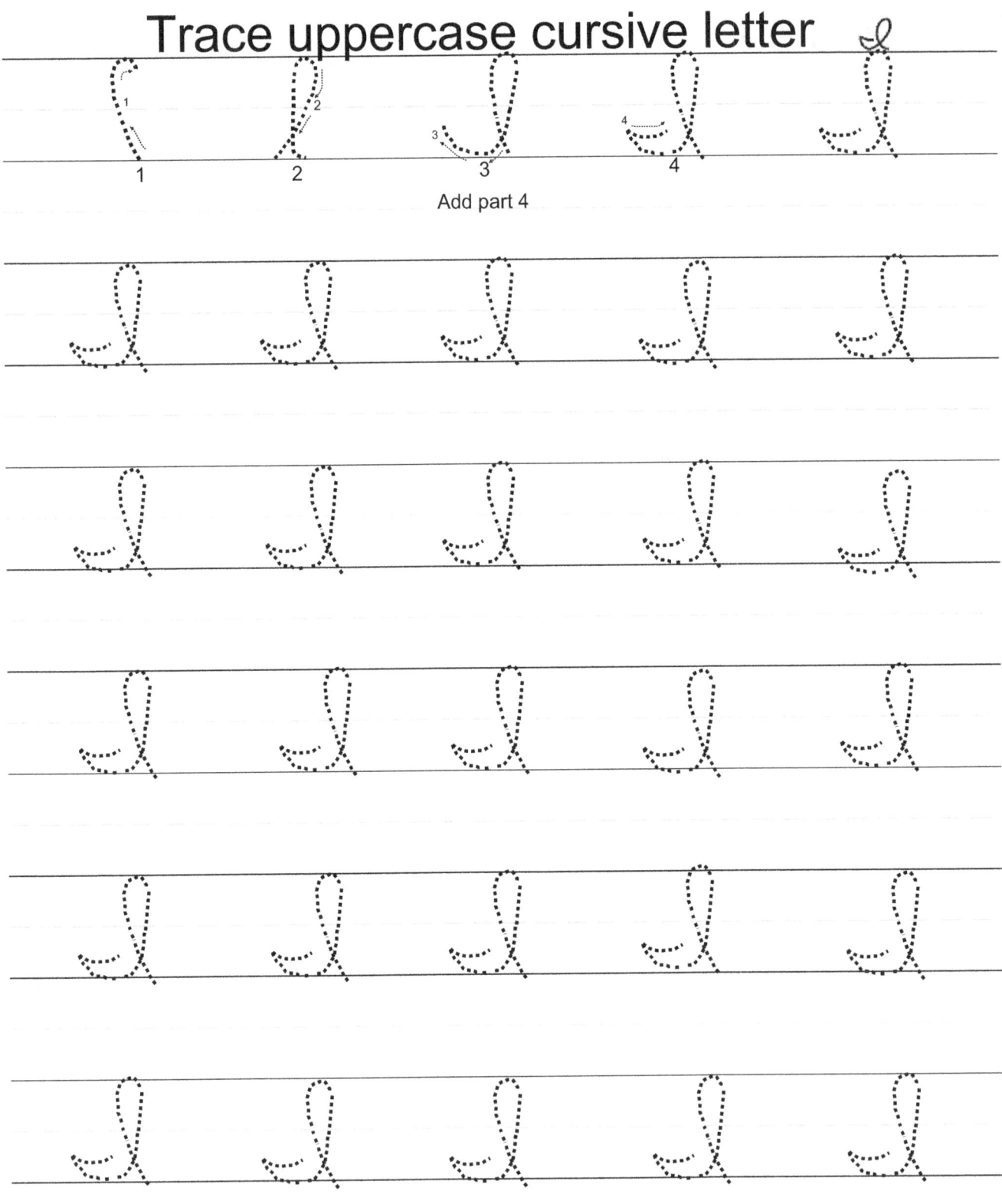

Trace this part of uppercase cursive letter

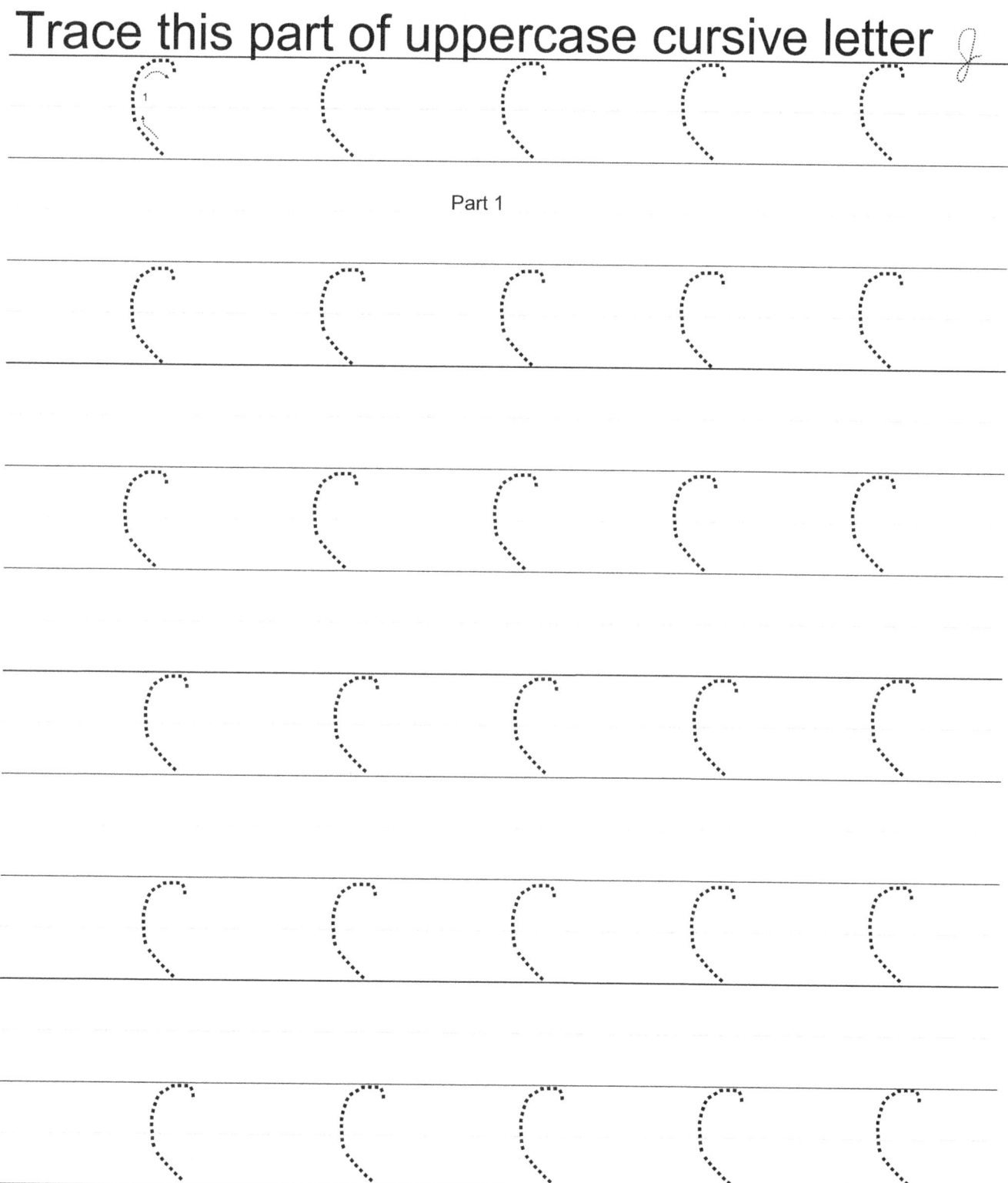

Part 1

31

Trace this part of uppercase cursive letter

Add part 2

32

Trace uppercase cursive letter J

Add part 3

Trace this part of uppercase cursive letter K

Part 1

Trace this part of uppercase cursive letter 𝒦

Add part 2

Trace uppercase cursive letter K

1   2   3

Add part 3

Trace this part of uppercase cursive letter $\mathscr{L}$

Part 1

Trace this part of uppercase cursive letter ℒ

1   2

Add part 2

Trace this part of uppercase cursive letter

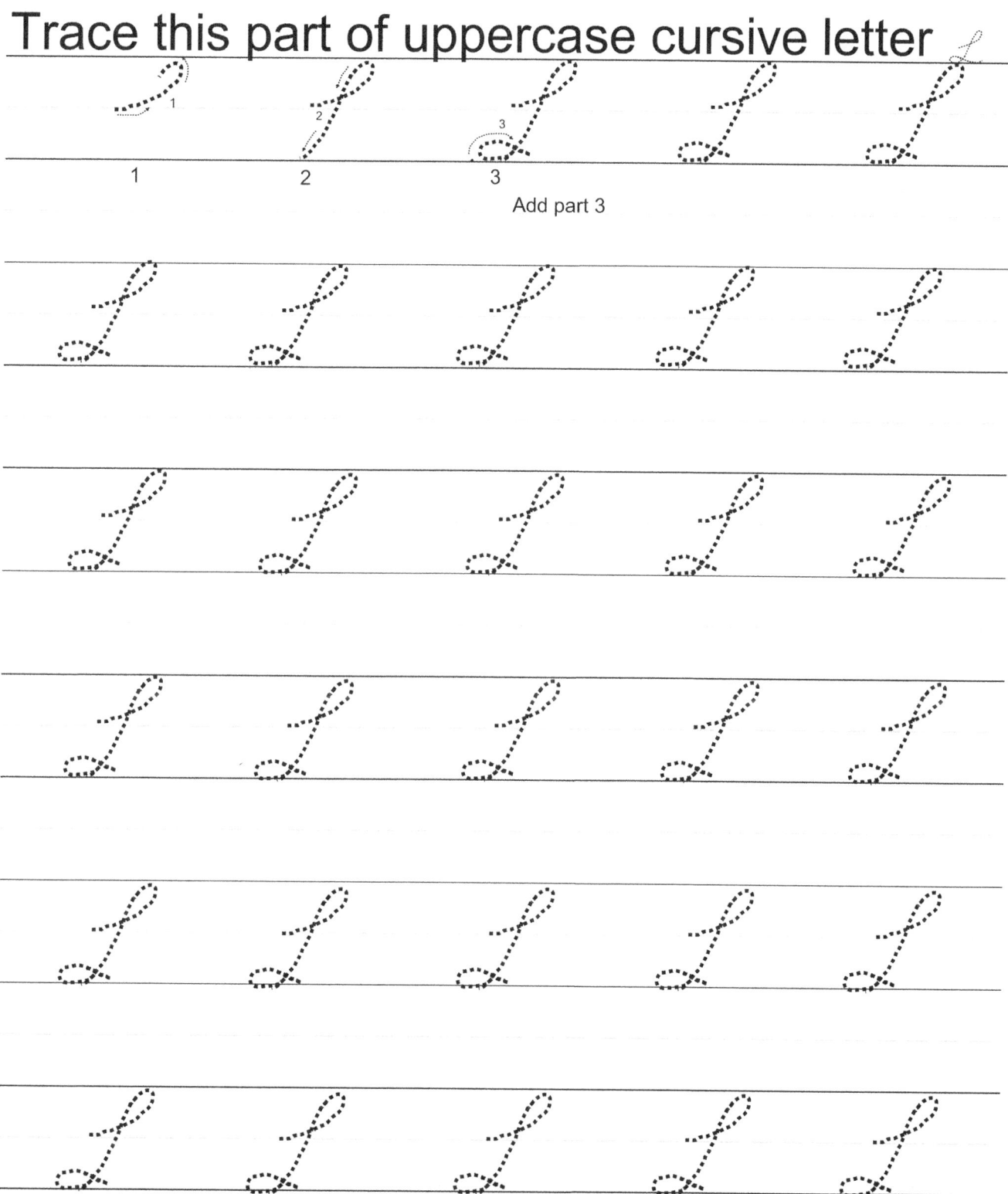

Add part 3

Trace uppercase cursive letter ℒ

Trace this part of uppercase cursive letter m

Part 1

Trace this part of uppercase cursive letter m

Add part 2

42

Trace uppercase cursive letter m

1   2   3
Add part 3

Trace this part of uppercase cursive letter 𝓃

Part 1

Trace uppercase cursive letter n

Add part 2

45

Trace this part of uppercase cursive letter O

Part 1

Trace uppercase cursive letter

Part 2

Trace this part of uppercase cursive letter 𝒫

Part 1

Trace this part of uppercase cursive letter 𝒫

Part 2

Trace uppercase cursive letter P

1   2   1 & 2

Add part 1 & 2

Trace this part of uppercase cursive letter 2

Part 1

Trace uppercase cursive letter 2

Add part 2

Trace this part of uppercase cursive letter R

Part 1
(R is made like P)

Trace this part of uppercase cursive letter R

Part 2
(R is made like P)

54

Trace uppercase cursive letter

1 2 1 & 2

Add part 3
(R is made like P)

Trace uppercase cursive letter R

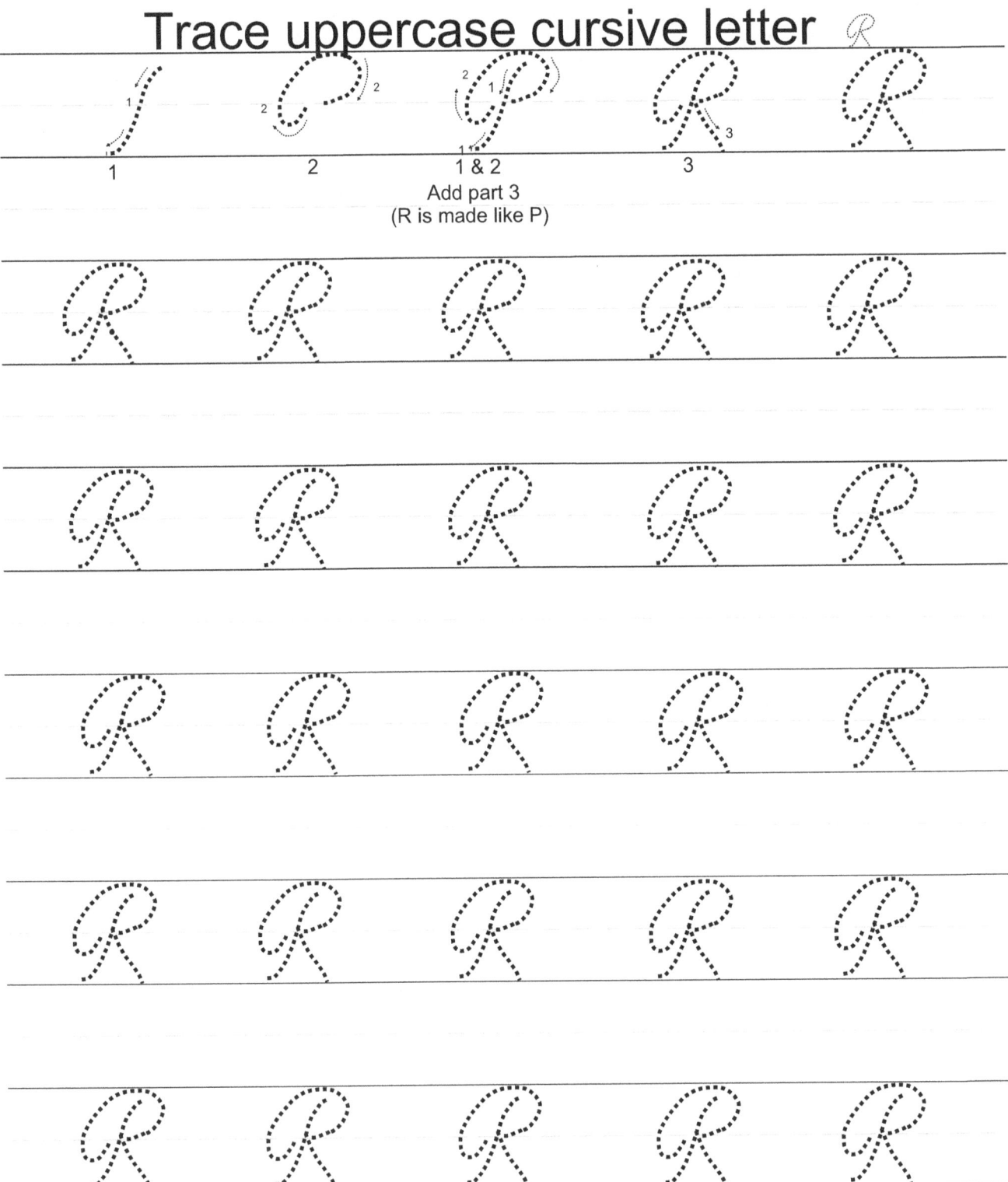

Trace this part of uppercase cursive letter

Part 1

Trace this part of uppercase cursive letter

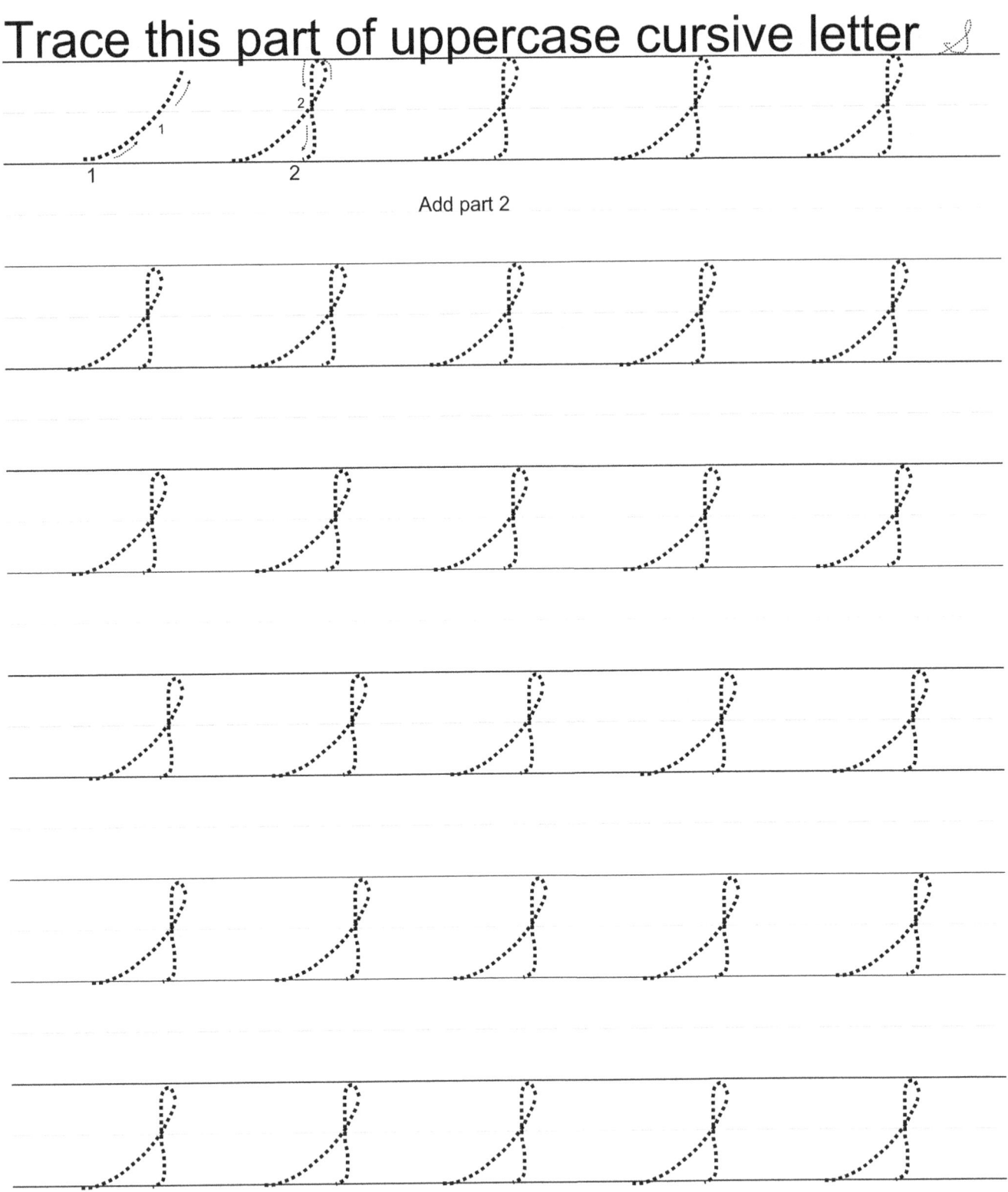

Add part 2

Trace uppercase cursive letter ℐ

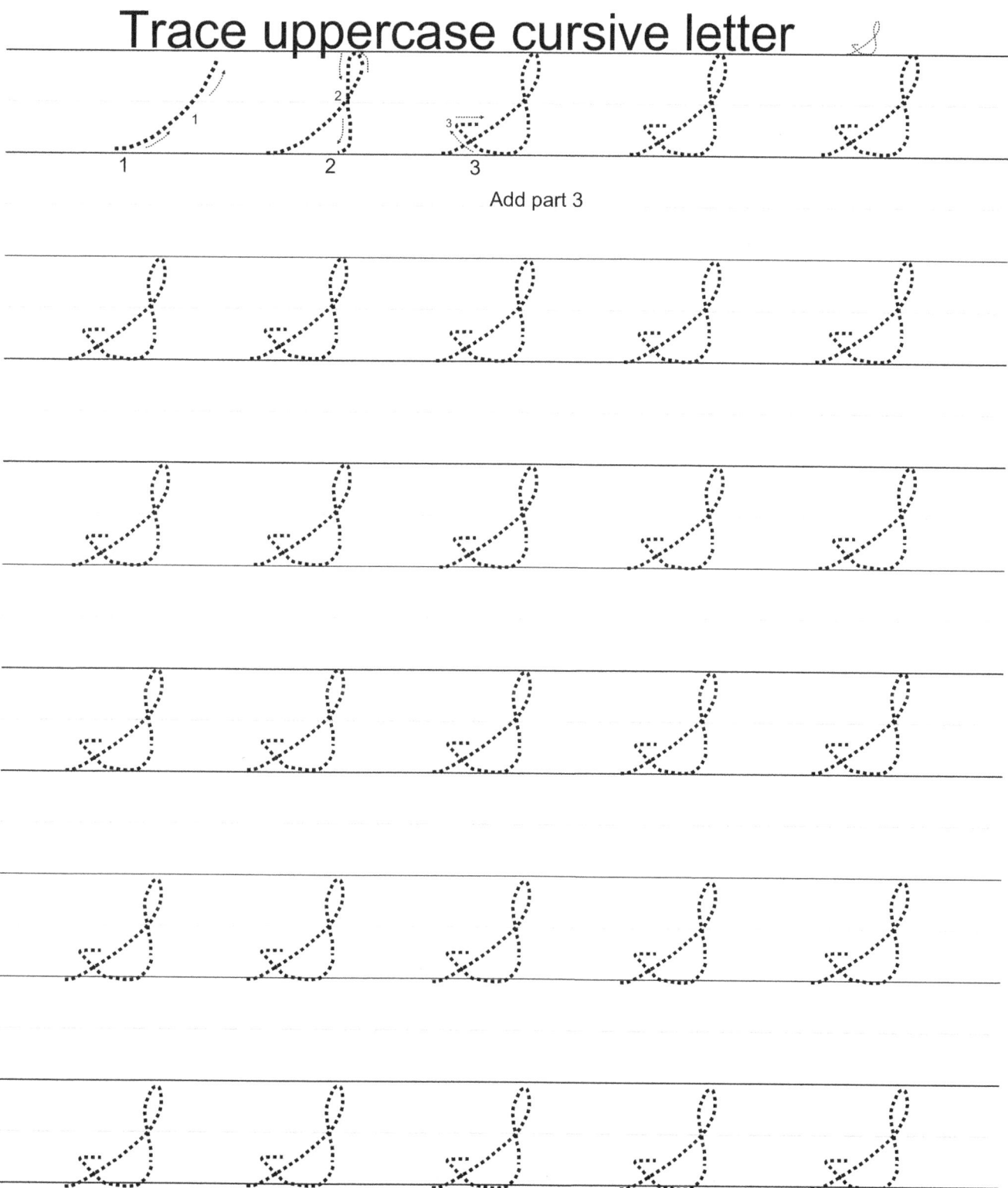

Add part 3

Trace this part of uppercase cursive letter J

Part 1

Trace uppercase cursive letter J

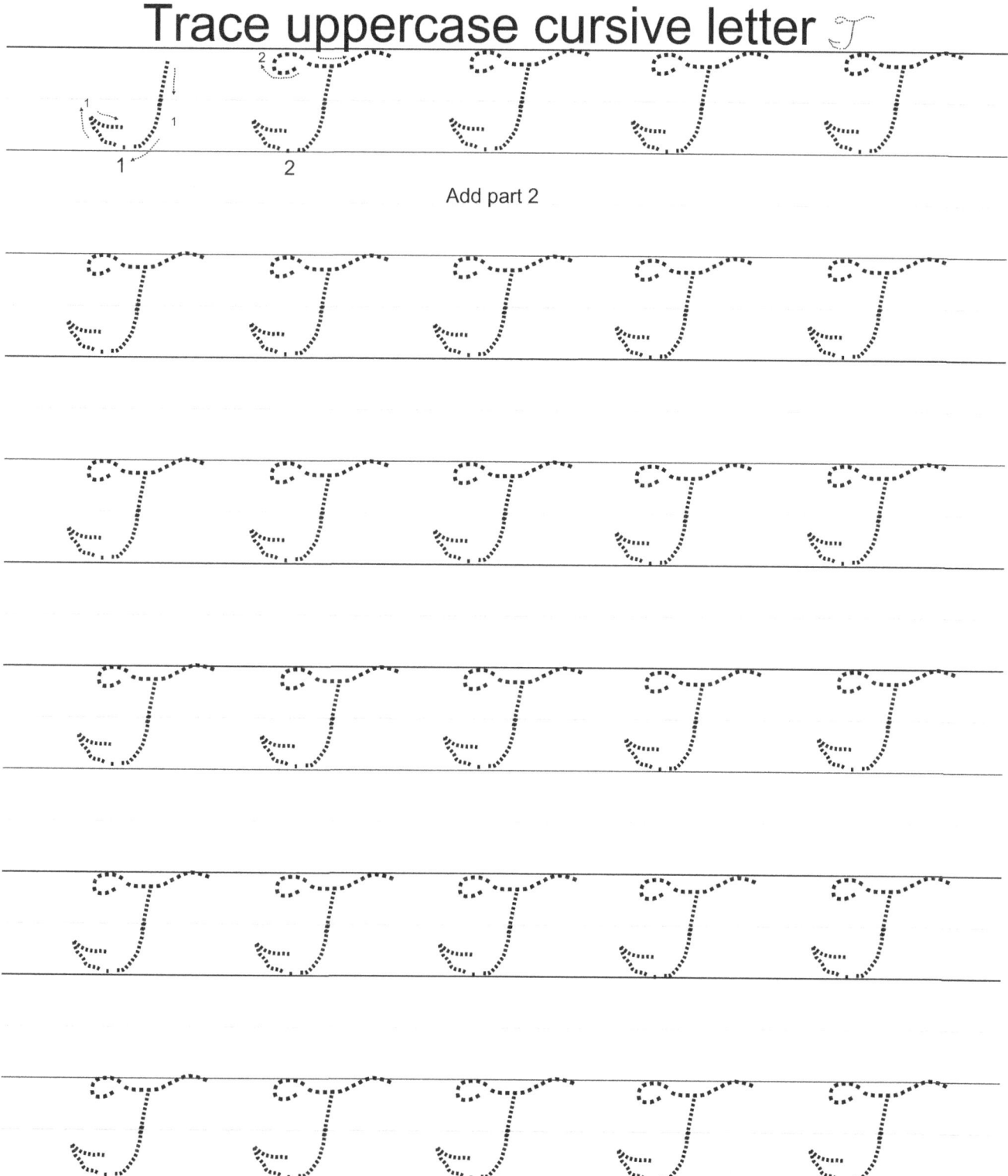

Add part 2

Trace this part of uppercase cursive letter $\mathcal{U}$

Part 1

Trace uppercase cursive letter U

Add part 2

Trace this part of uppercase cursive letter

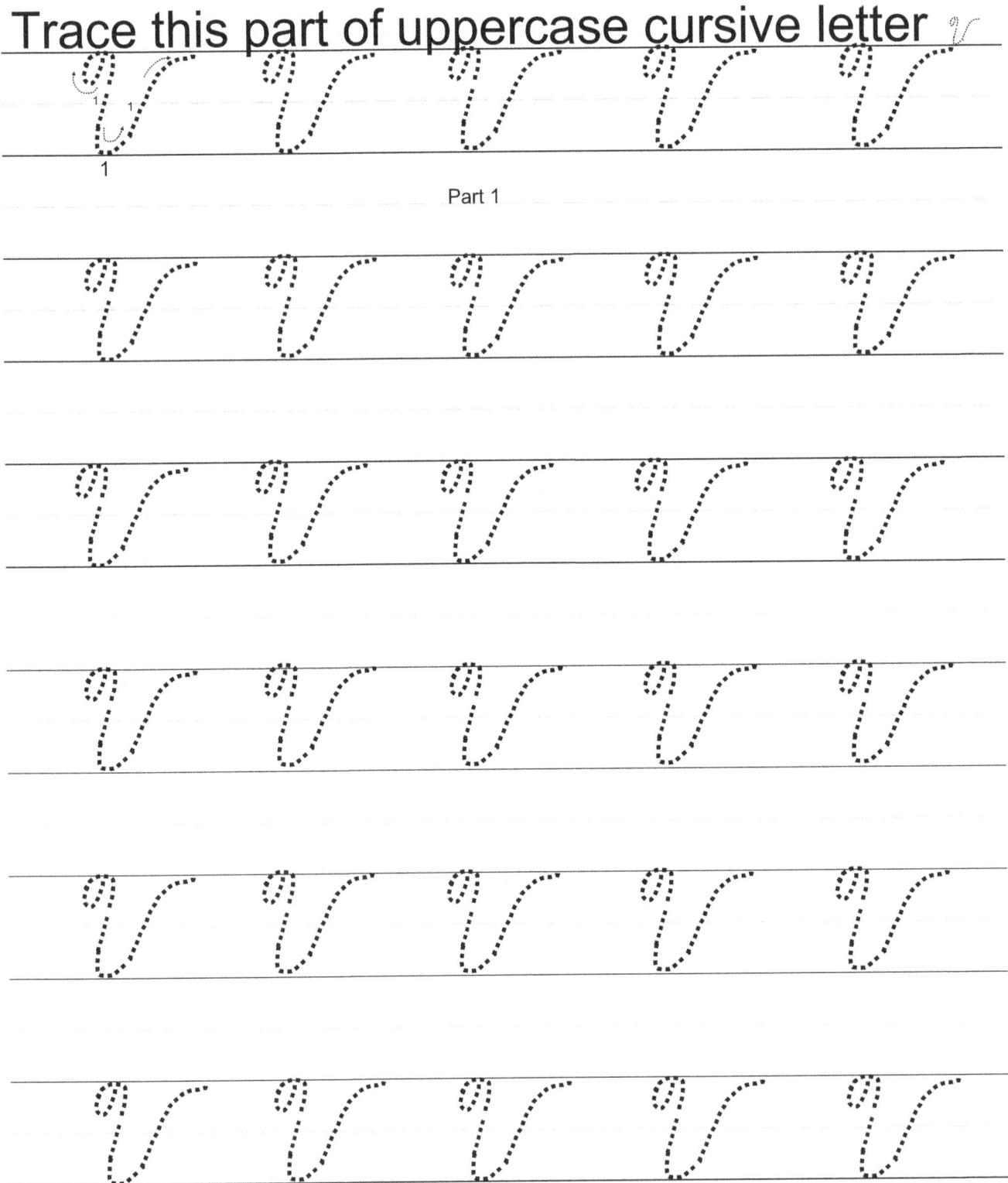

Part 1

64

Trace this part of uppercase cursive letter W

Part 1

Trace this part of uppercase cursive letter 𝒱

1   2

Add part 2

Trace this part of uppercase cursive letter И

1 2 3
Add part 3

Trace uppercase cursive letter W

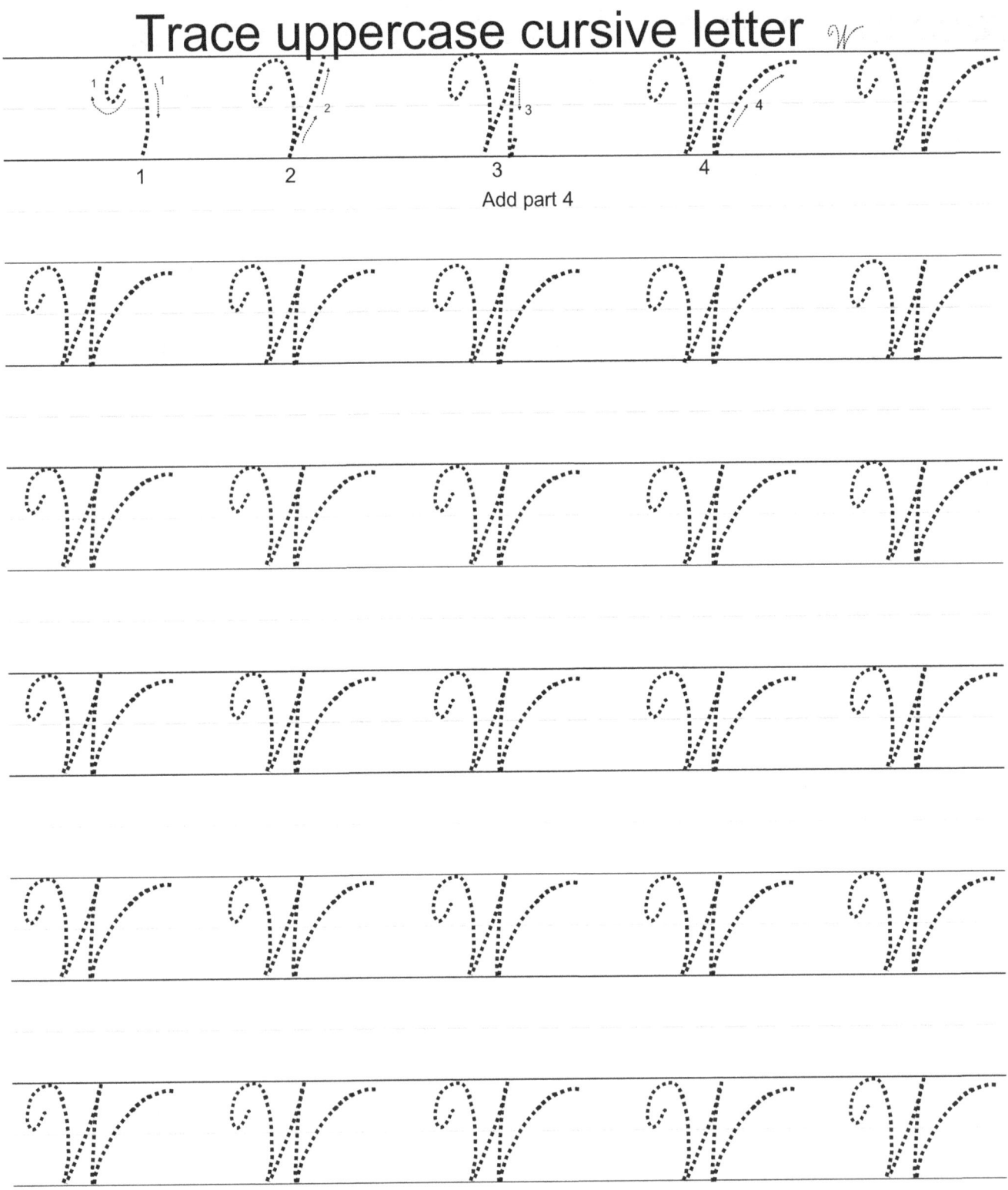

Add part 4

Trace this part of uppercase cursive letter X

Part 1

Trace uppercase cursive letter X

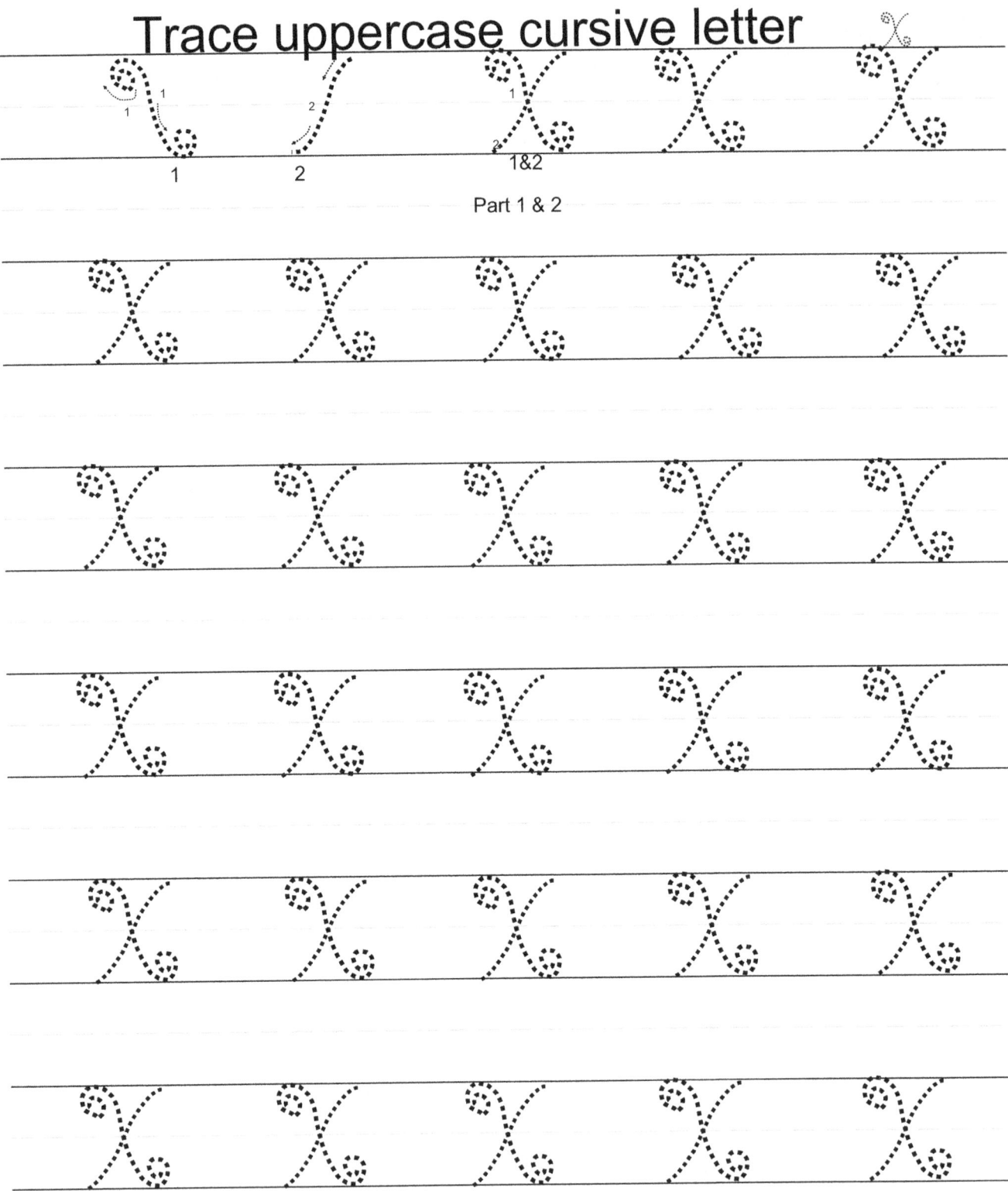

Part 1 & 2

Trace this part of uppercase cursive letter

Part 1

71

Trace this part of uppercase cursive letter Y

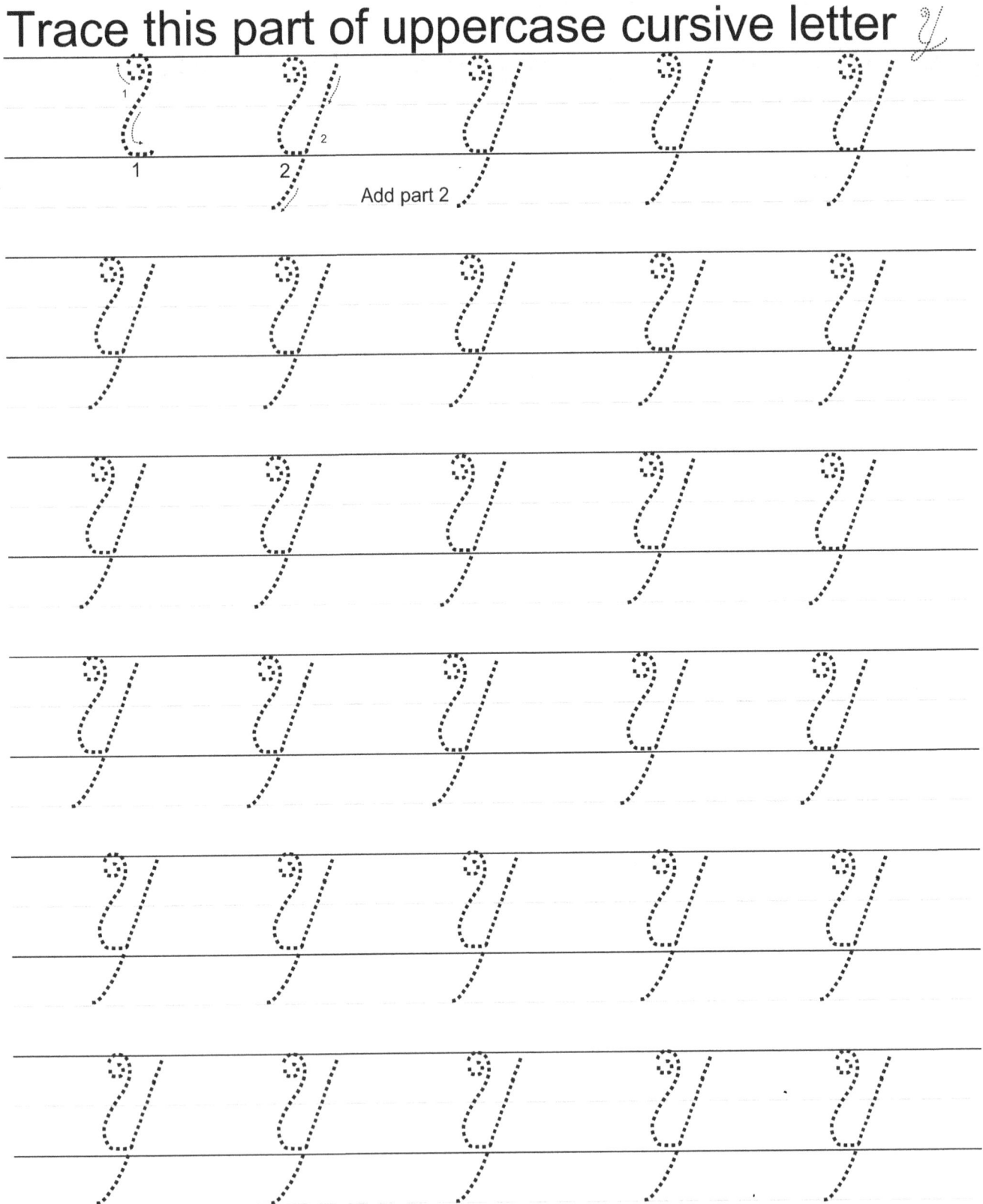

Add part 2

72

Trace uppercase cursive letter Y

Trace this part of uppercase cursive letter 𝒴

Part 1

Trace this part of uppercase cursive letter $\mathcal{J}$

1 2

Add part 2

Trace this part of uppercase cursive letter $\mathcal{G}$

1   2   3

Add part 3

Trace uppercase crusive letter $\mathcal{G}$

Add part 4

Made in the USA
Monee, IL
30 May 2024

58695090R00044